Family Planning

A Guide for Exploring the Issues

Charles and Elizabeth Balsam

Revised Edition

One Liguori Drive
Liguori, Missouri 63057
(314) 464-2500

Imprimi Potest:
John F. Dowd, C.SS.R.
Provincial, St. Louis Province
Redemptorist Fathers

Imprimatur:
+ Edward J. O'Donnell
Vicar General, Archdiocese of St. Louis

ISBN 0-89243-238-1

Copyright © 1985, Liguori Publications
Printed in U.S.A.
All rights reserved.

Revised 1986

Excerpts from THE DOCUMENTS OF VATICAN II, Abbott-Gallagher edition, have been reprinted with permission of America Press, Inc., 106 West 56th Street, New York, NY 10019. Copyright © 1966. All rights reserved.

The Scripture text Genesis 1:31 is taken from the NEW AMERICAN BIBLE, copyright © 1970, by the Confraternity of Christian Doctrine, Washington, DC, and are used by permission of copyright owner. All rights reserved.

Excerpts from TO LIVE IN CHRIST JESUS, copyright ©1976, ON THE FAMILY, copyright © 1981, and ON THE REGULATION OF BIRTH, copyright ©1968, by the United States Catholic Conference are used with permission.

Many Thanks

There are many people who helped us write and revise this booklet. Space does not allow us to mention them all. However, we would like to express our sincere appreciation and indebtedness to three special, supportive people: Rev. Albert Moraczewski, O.P.; Joseph M. Boyle, Ph.D.; and most especially Hanna Klaus, M.D., F.A.C.O.G.

Contents

Cooperating with God	4
Knowing the Facts	5
Family Planning Methods	7
Natural Family Planning	9
A Woman's Perspective	12
Artificial Methods	15
Methods Which Are Not Reliable	21
A Word About Effectiveness	22
For Men Only	25
A Shared Decision, A Shared Responsibility	29
What Does the Catholic Church Teach?	32
Seeking the Truth and Embracing It	40
Worksheet	46
Other Resources and Suggested Reading	47
Resource Centers for Further Information	48
Local/Diocesan NFP Information	48

Cooperating with God

"In its most profound reality, love is essentially a gift; and conjugal love . . . does not end with the couple, because it makes them capable of the greatest possible gift, the gift by which they become cooperators with God for giving life to a new human person."[1]

Is the love that you have for each other a gift capable of an even greater gift, that of transmitting new life?

Being "cooperators with God" involves much more than simply biological information and technological research because family planning is a faith issue. Cooperating with God is related to your perception of how God acts through you as embodied spirits.

Being "cooperators with God" also reflects your understanding of the covenant commitment of two persons in Christian marriage. We believe, therefore, that it is essential that you obtain and discuss — as a couple — accurate information about family planning.

Whether you are Catholic or not, there are many factors besides religion that surround the question of family planning. Other factors, such as health risks and side effects, must be considered. But we also want to challenge you to think about your family planning goals, shared responsibility, the gift of fertility, and the joy of having children — not just how to avoid having them.

Notes

1. Pope John Paul II, *On the Family* (The Apostolic Exhortation *Familiaris Consortio*), 1981, Part Two, 14.

Knowing the Facts

In our teaching experience, we encounter many couples who are ignorant of the most basic information about family planning methods. Many times a decision to use a particular method is made quickly, with little knowledge, understanding, or reflection. This reality has urged us to include an explanation of all family planning methods in this booklet. An explanation does not imply endorsement, however. Later in the booklet we give reasons for our views and express our support of Catholic teaching concerning the moral and relational values of responsible parenthood.

Because of the potentially serious health risks of some contraceptives, doctors are required by law to provide women with a government brochure on the oral contraceptive and the intrauterine device (IUD) when they seek to use those methods. Regrettably, the government brochure and the vital information it contains are sometimes ignored or given little attention. Despite the doctors' responsibility, the bottom line is that patients are ultimately responsible for themselves. Doctors cannot necessarily be blamed for complications resulting from the use of the Pill when patients are supposed to be aware of the risk they may be undertaking.

Some doctors or family planning agencies may not have up-to-date information about natural methods. As a result, clients may only receive information on contraceptive methods. Here again you are responsible for finding out many of these things for yourself. In her book *The Personal Fertility Guide,* Terrie Guay says it well: " . . . until all the facts are known and understood a woman is not free to make an informed choice. Ignorance is never a virtue, and choices depend not only on values but also on knowledge."[1]

This booklet provides you with an opportunity to educate yourself in an area that can affect your physical, emotional, and marital well-being. Because some contraceptives may be harmful to a person, it is important to understand all of the consequences involved with any method. The most recent, up-to-date information has been compiled here in a format that attempts to be informative, understandable, and challenging. *Please note:* This booklet is by no means exhaustive nor a substitute for the more detailed information that can be obtained from your doctor or natural family planning professional.

Notes

1. Terrie Guay, *The Personal Fertility Guide*. Harbor Publishing, Inc., San Francisco, CA, 1980, pp. ix-x.

Family Planning Methods

To begin with, methods of family planning fall into two basic categories: *natural* and *artificial*.

Natural methods do not use any chemical, drug, or device. They rely, rather, on the natural signs and symptoms within a woman to identify the times of fertility and infertility. The natural process of the reproductive system(s) is left intact and undisturbed.

Modern methods of natural family planning (NFP) differ from Calendar Rhythm in this way: they are based upon the physiological signs of fertility and infertility as they occur in each and every cycle.

With a natural method, if you wish to avoid pregnancy you mutually agree as a couple to refrain from intercourse at the time of fertility. On the other hand, if you wish to achieve pregnancy you continue using the method and plan intercourse at the most fertile time.

Artificial methods rely on a device, a chemical, or a drug to change and/or interfere with the normal process of the reproductive system(s) and therefore prevent pregnancy.

The name *contraceptive* (which means a preventive to conception) is in some cases a misnomer. With the oral contraceptive and the intrauterine device, *conception is not always prevented*. Instead, the human embryo is unable to survive in the disturbed uterus as a result of the device or drug.

Artificial methods are not intended to help achieve pregnancy. If a pregnancy is desired, an artificial method must be discontinued.

The chart that follows is a very simplified outline of the various family planning methods.

Method	Effectiveness* Method	Effectiveness* User-Variable	Physical Side Effects and Health Risks
Billings/Ovulation (natural)	98-99%	85-90%	none
Sympto-Thermal (natural)	98-99%	85-90%	none
Oral Contraceptive (the Pill)	99%	96-98%	breast tenderness, nausea, vomiting, break-through bleeding, headaches, depression, weight change, abnormal sugar metabolism, cystitis, high blood pressure, heart attack, stroke, blood clots, gall bladder disease, liver tumors
Intrauterine Device (IUD) NOTE: All intrauterine devices (IUDs) except one have recently been removed from the U.S. market	99%	95-98%	heavy menstrual bleed, cramps, painful intercourse, anemia, break-through bleeding, pelvic infection, blood poisoning, perforation of the uterus, septic abortion, ectopic pregnancy
Diaphragm (with spermicide)	97-98%	80-90%	irritation or allergic reaction to rubber and/or spermicide, bladder infection
Spermicides (cream, jelly, foam, suppository)	97-98%	80-90%	irritation or allergic reaction to chemicals, bladder infection
Condom (prophylactic, rubber)	98%	80-90%	irritation or allergic reaction to rubber material

*Data on effectiveness of family planning methods taken from: Johns Hopkins University, *Population Reports*, Series M, Number 9, November-December, 1985; and *Natural Family Planning: A Review*, "Obstetrical and Gynecological Survey, 1982," The Williams & Wilkins Co. Refer to pages 22-24 of this booklet for a fuller explanation of this idea.

Natural Family Planning

Billings/Ovulation Method

The Ovulation Method of natural family planning is sometimes called the Billings Method (for Drs. John and Evelyn Billings of Australia). This method teaches a couple to identify the fertile and infertile days in a woman's cycle by observing the changes in the cervical mucus discharge.

The cervix is at the base of a woman's uterus. Mucus is discharged from the cervix directly prior to and at the time of ovulation.

Daily, the couple using the Ovulation Method keeps a chart of the woman's vaginal sensations and the color and consistency of any mucus discharge. The sensations and type of mucus observed tell the woman when she is fertile. If pregnancy is to be avoided, continence (refraining from intercourse) is necessary during the fertile days of the cycle. Continence is a mutual effort for both the man and the woman of which neither partner has to bear the sole responsibility for avoiding pregnancy.

It is necessary to learn the Ovulation Method from an instructor (often a couple) who is qualified to teach the method and who has personal experience with it.

The Ovulation Method can be used successfully in any reproductive situation: regular, irregular, or anovular cycles; while breast-feeding; and during premenopause.

Method Effectiveness: 98-99%

Side Effects: None

Health Factors: None

Effect on Ability to Have Children: Because the Ovulation Method does not use any drugs, devices, or chemicals, it leaves the reproductive system of both the male and female undisturbed and does not endanger the fertility of the couple. Since the Ovulation Method identifies the time of fertility, it can be used in an effort to achieve pregnancy (as well as to avoid pregnancy). For couples who have "low fertility" or some difficulty in conceiving, the Ovulation Method may be helpful to achieving pregnancy.

Sympto-Thermal Method

The Sympto-Thermal Method of natural family planning combines the use of the Ovulation Method with the basal body temperature and other indicators of fertility. The cervical mucus is observed and, upon waking in the morning, the woman takes a temperature reading with a special calibrated thermometer.

A woman's basal body temperature rises after ovulation. When it has remained high for three consecutive days, this fact signals that the fertile phase of the cycle has passed.

With the Sympto-Thermal Method some aspects of Calendar Rhythm may also be used, and actual changes in the cervix may be observed and noted. At times the basal body temperature may have limited use — for example, when cycles are anovular or irregular; during months when breast-feeding is done; or during premenopause. In such situations observation of the cervical mucus is very important.

With the Sympto-Thermal Method, continence (refraining from intercourse) during the fertile time is necessary to avoid pregnancy.

Instruction by a qualified teacher is essential to learn the method.

The Sympto-Thermal Method can be used successfully in any reproductive situation: with regular, irregular, or anovular cycles; during the time of breast-feeding; during premenopause.

Method Effectiveness: 98-99%

Side Effects: None

Health Factors: None

Effect on Ability to Have Children: Because the Sympto-Thermal Method does not disturb or endanger the fertility of the couple, there is no adverse effect on the ability to have children. By observing the cervical mucus discharge, a couple can identify the time of fertility and actually use this knowledge to achieve pregnancy. For couples who have difficulty in conceiving, this information may be helpful to achieving pregnancy.

A Woman's Perspective
by Elizabeth Balsam

"God looked at everything he had made, and he found it very good."

(Genesis 1:31)

When I first began learning about natural family planning some years ago, I did so out of curiosity as a nature lover. At that time, NFP seemed to fit in well with my love for the outdoors and my appreciation of God's creation. I do not remember when it finally struck me that I was also part of that marvelous creation. I gradually grew into the realization that God had implanted in me my uniqueness as a woman. Spiritually, the mystery of my fertility was as close to God and nature as I could get. I eventually thought that using anything other than a natural method in my marriage would be similar to pouring tons of pollutants into a river. Given my love of nature, I could not "pollute" my body, my self.

Other women have a similar experience of NFP; but, just as each woman is different, so are the stories they tell. The beauty of a natural method is that it allows every woman to be the unique person she is. I do not have to alter myself or my fertility in order to be "normal" or to be accepted by my husband.

The most common hesitancy among couples to using NFP is the continence required in order to avoid conception. While this is a very important reality of natural methods and one that should not be ignored, continence itself can be an advantage. Nona Aguilar reports that "many women specifically mentioned how much it meant to them that their husbands were willing to abstain for the sake of their mutual goals."[1] The shared responsibility and mutual commitment for family planning through the use of NFP has been a source of great satisfaction for many women.

If this is what a woman experiences, what about her husband? Nona Aguilar states: " . . . husbands reported themselves pleased by the mutuality, closeness, sharing, and equality that are an intrinsic part of natural family planning. . . . "[2] Continence is simply accepted as a necessary part of NFP in order to enjoy its full advantages. In my own marriage, my husband's determination to make NFP "work" did more to bring us close together than I ever would have expected.

The most exciting advantage of NFP, I feel, is sometimes too easily overlooked. Using NFP to achieve pregnancy is almost an afterthought, something not seen as an integral part of the whole NFP picture. In our sincere efforts to prove natural methods "successful" (to friends, relatives, and doctors) we sometimes can forget about the gift of our potential to have children. Eventually, though, "It is not unusual for couples [who use NFP] to be so enchanted by the way that nature works that they consciously choose to have a child."[3] The man, who is constantly fertile, brings his seed to his fertile wife, and together they share this awesome potential to begin a new life.

Mary Shivanandan, an expert in family enrichment and sex education, says that for some couples NFP releases a "deep wellspring of creativity."[4] Natural family planning does not hide nor cover up this creative and loving potential. It brings it out into the open. For a woman, pregnancy itself seems to bring a sense of oneness with the creative intentions of God. I remember one woman explaining that she and her husband were tremendously happy with their three children and did not plan to have any more. But she would not allow herself to close the door totally. "Who knows how we will feel in the future?" she smiled. She could not bring herself to call their baby "our last child." For now he was simply the youngest.

With time, I have come to understand that fertility acceptance through NFP can encompass a wide range of situations. For many couples, the knowledge and use of a natural method helps them effectively avoid or achieve a pregnancy as they wish. It is a shining example of true family planning. Such couples are understandably proud of their successful efforts with NFP.

For some couples, unfortunately, fertility acceptance may mean dealing with infertility (either temporary or permanent). While NFP can sometimes be of help to those who have "low" fertility, more serious problems often need medical attention. Eventually, infertility may present a challenge to consider adoption, foster care, or other forms of parenthood as a way of sharing in the creative intentions of God.

Finally, fertility acceptance may mean welcoming a "surprise" pregnancy and allowing God's plan to reveal itself through the child. (*No method* is 100% effective in preventing pregnancy.) As one woman pointed out, all children are gifts no matter how they come.

God has generously provided us with the gift of fertility and the ability to understand and embrace it. Fertility is an integral part of God's complementary design of man and woman. God, I am sure, is proud of this creation of man and woman. After all, he did find it "very good."

Notes

1. Nona Aguilar, *No-Pill, No-Risk Birth Control*. Rawson, Wade Publishers, Inc., New York, NY, 1980, p. 81.
2. Ibid., p. 82.
3. Mary Shivanandan, *Challenge to Love*. KM Associates, Bethesda, MD, 1979, p. 74.
4. Ibid., p. 76.

Artificial Methods

Oral Contraceptives

The "Pill" refers to any of the oral contraceptives. The most widely used pill contains two synthetic female hormones, estrogen and progestin, and is taken twenty-one days each month. Another, sometimes called the "mini-pill," contains only progestin and is taken continuously.

The pills must be taken regularly and exactly as instructed. The contraceptive Pill is a prescription drug.

For the most part, the Pill prevents ovulation from occurring in the woman. It also causes a thick mucus at the cervix which acts as a barrier to sperm. In the case where ovulation does occur and the sperm do penetrate the mucus, conception may result. Due to the hostile environment that the Pill creates in the womb, however, the human embryo may be unable to implant in the wall of the uterus. (The result may be a very early abortion indistinguishable from a normal menstrual flow. In this, the woman is unaware that she is even pregnant.)

A woman using the Pill is advised to have a pap test about every six months.

Method Effectiveness: 99%

Side Effects: Side effects may include breast tenderness, nausea or vomiting, gain or loss of weight, unexpected vaginal bleeding, and higher levels of sugar and fat in the blood. Although it happens infrequently, use of the Pill can cause blood clots (in the legs and, less frequently, in the lungs, brain, or heart). A clot that reaches the lungs, or forms in the brain or heart, can be fatal. Pill users have a greater risk of heart attack and stroke than nonusers. This risk increases with age and is greater if the Pill user smokes. Some Pill users tend to develop high blood pressure, but it is usually mild and may be reversed by discontinuing use of the Pill. A rare but potentially serious side effect is benign liver tumors that can rupture, causing fatal hemorrhage.

Health Factors: Women who smoke should not use the Pill because smoking increases the risk of heart attack or stroke. Other women who should not take the Pill are those who have had a heart attack, stroke, angina pectoris, blood clots, cancer of the breast or uterus, or scanty or irregular periods. A woman who believes she may be pregnant should not take the Pill because it increases the risk of defect of the baby. Health problems such as migraine headaches, mental depression, fibroids of the uterus, heart or kidney disease, asthma, high blood pressure, diabetes, or epilepsy may be made worse by the use of the Pill. Risks with the Pill increase with age; as a woman enters her late thirties many doctors advise her to discontinue using it.

Effect on Ability to Have Children: When a woman stops taking the Pill in order to become pregnant, there may be a delay before she is actually able to become pregnant. To allow the woman's reproductive system to return to normal, a couple should wait a short time — three to six months — after stopping the Pill before attempting to become pregnant.

After childbirth, studies have shown that the drugs in the Pill appear in the breast milk of nursing mothers. The long-range effect on the infant is not known.

Intrauterine Device (IUD)

(NOTE: All IUDs, except one, have recently been removed from the U.S. market.) The intrauterine device (IUD) is a small plastic or metal device that is placed in the uterus of the woman through the cervical canal.

Insertion by a physician is necessary. After insertion, no further care is needed except to see that the device remains in place. The user can check herself, but she should be checked at least once a year by her doctor.

The IUD may cause pain or discomfort when inserted, and afterwards may cause cramps and a menstrual flow that is heavier than usual.

Since the IUD does not prevent ovulation from occurring, conception could be happening in almost every cycle. The IUD seems to interfere in some manner with the implantation of the human embryo in the wall of the uterus. (The result may be a very early abortion indistinguishable from a normal menstrual flow. In this, the woman is unaware that she is even pregnant.)

Method Effectiveness: 99%

Side Effects: IUD users may experience heavy menstrual bleeding, cramps, and painful intercourse. Major complications, which are infrequent, include anemia, pregnancy outside of the uterus, pelvic infections, perforation of the uterus or cervix, and septic abortion. A woman who experiences very heavy or irregular bleeding while using the IUD should consult her physician; removal of the IUD may be necessary to prevent anemia. Women susceptible to pelvic infection are more prone to infection while using the IUD. Serious complications can occur if the woman becomes pregnant while using the IUD; cases of blood poisoning, miscarriage, and even death have been reported. An IUD user who believes she may be pregnant should consult her doctor immediately. If pregnancy is confirmed, the IUD may have to be removed. Although it rarely happens, the IUD can pierce the wall of the uterus while it is being inserted, with the result that surgery is required to remove it. The risk of tubal pregnancy is greater with the use of the IUD, and the risk increases the longer the IUD is used.

Health Factors: Before having the IUD inserted, a woman should tell her doctor if she has had any of the following: cancer or other abnormalities of the uterus or cervix; bleeding between periods or heavy menstrual flow; infection of the uterus, cervix, or pelvis; prior IUD use; recent pregnancy; abortion or miscarriage; uterine surgery; venereal disease; severe menstrual cramps; allergy to copper; anemia; fainting attacks; unexplained genital bleeding or vaginal discharge; suspicious or abnormal pap test.

Effect on Ability to Have Children: Pelvic infection in some IUD users may result in their future inability to have children.

Diaphragm (with spermicide)

The diaphragm is a shallow cup of thin rubber stretched over a flexible ring. Before intercourse a sperm-killing cream, jelly, or foam is put on both sides of the Diaphragm, which the woman then places inside the vagina. The Diaphragm covers the opening of the uterus, at the cervix, thus preventing the sperm from entering the uterus. The spermicide also helps to disable and destroy the sperm.

Sizing and fitting of the Diaphragm must be done by a doctor, and requires yearly checkups. Size and fit should also be checked if the woman gains or loses more than ten pounds, and after childbirth or miscarriage.

Method Effectiveness: 97-98%

Side Effects: There may be an allergic reaction to the rubber of the diaphragm or to the spermicide. Some irritation may occur. There is an increased susceptibility to bladder infection.

Health Factors: None

Effect on Ability to Have Children: None

Spermicides

Several brands of vaginal foam, cream, jelly, or suppositories can be used alone, without a diaphragm. They must be placed inside the vagina before intercourse. At the opening of the uterus, spermicides form a barrier that prevents sperm from reaching the egg. Spermicides disable, damage, and destroy the sperm.

No prescription is necessary for the purchase of spermicides.

Some brands of spermicides are not as effective as others in preventing pregnancy. For example, instead of foaming up, some suppositories may remain intact and fall out of the vagina. The aerosol foams are the most effective of the chemical spermicides.

Method Effectiveness: 97-98%

Side Effects: Some burning or irritation of the vagina or penis may occur due to an allergic reaction to the chemicals in spermicides. There is an increased susceptibility to bladder infection.

Health Factors: None

Effect on Ability to Have Children: None

Condom

The condom is a thin sheath of rubber or processed lamb cecum that fits over the penis. The condom must be fit in place over the penis before any genital contact with the woman.

No prescription is required for the purchase of condoms.

The condom prevents the sperm from entering the woman's vagina so that it cannot fertilize the egg. Care must be taken in the use of the condom since it can slip or tear during use or sperm can spill from the condom upon withdrawal from the vagina.

Method Effectiveness: 98%

Side Effects: Occasionally, there may be an allergic reaction to the rubber material, causing some irritation.

Health Factors: None

Effect on Ability to Have Children: None

Methods Which Are Not Reliable

1. Douching after intercourse is unreliable as a means of avoiding pregnancy. If the conditions are favorable in the woman's body, sperm can travel to meet the egg within minutes of ejaculation.

2. Not all forms of breast-feeding provide for extended infertility after childbirth. In general, breast-feeding may delay the return of fertility in many women, but certain kinds of breast-feeding ("partial") do little to suppress ovulation. In some cases, a nursing mother could conceive within several months of delivery. (NOTE: The return of fertility after childbirth depends greatly on the *type* of breast-feeding/mothering used. Some forms of breast-feeding ["total" or "ecological"] more completely suppress ovulation for an extended length of time.)

3. *Coitus interruptus* is the difficult and often frustrating practice of withdrawing the penis from the vagina just before ejaculation. It is unreliable as a means of avoiding pregnancy because a few drops of very potent fluid may leave the penis before ejaculation and before withdrawal.

4. For most women, Calendar Rhythm is not a reliable way to avoid pregnancy because some irregularity may occur in a woman's cycles. Calendar Rhythm is based on calculations from previous cycles with no regard for the present one. A woman could conceive at a time when she thinks she is infertile.

A Word About Effectiveness

There is some confusion among couples and medical professionals alike about the effectiveness of natural methods of family planning. Many still think of natural methods as only Calendar Rhythm or, possibly, Basal Body Temperature. Nona Aguilar, in her book *No-Pill, No-Risk Birth Control*, sums it up well: "Natural family planning is not well known in the United States. Its reliability is unpublished, little recognized and usually confused with . . . calendar rhythm."[1]

Confusion, ignorance, and misinformation about the effectiveness of modern methods of natural family planning mean that many couples never give it serious consideration. This is very unfortunate, not only because natural methods are, in fact, reliable, but because they can do so much to enrich a marriage.

On page 8 of this booklet, statistics for "method effectiveness" are given for both natural and artificial methods. A method effectiveness rate is determined by the number of pregnancies which occur in proportion to the total number of couples using that method even when the rules for pregnancy avoidance have been properly understood and faithfully followed.

Method effectiveness figures are usually high, illustrating the reliability of the method *when used correctly* to avoid pregnancy. Keep in mind that *none of the methods listed in this booklet are 100% effective* in avoiding pregnancy. All methods carry some slight possibility of pregnancy even when they are used strictly according to the guidelines.

Besides the slight possibility of a pregnancy occurring when a method is used correctly, pregnancies during use of a family planning method can also occur for other reasons:

1. the couple does not understand how to use a method;
2. the couple knows how to use a method but disregards the rules for avoiding pregnancy;
3. the couple wants to achieve pregnancy.

Number 3 above applies only to the actual use of natural methods of family planning. Artificial methods are intended solely for the avoidance of pregnancy and cannot help you achieve pregnancy. On the other hand, natural methods can be used either to avoid *or* to achieve pregnancy. The complete and accurate definition of true family planning, which obviously includes having children, is more fully realized in natural methods.

The percentage rates for "user-variable effectiveness" (see the chart on page 8) for both natural and artificial methods are determined by the number of pregnancies which occur in proportion to the total number of couples using that method under the circumstances described in numbers 1 and 2 above. Number 1 above means that pregnancies may occur because the couple did not seek or receive proper instruction in how to use a method. This does not mean that the method is unreliable, but that the couple did not have correct information about how properly to use the method to avoid pregnancy.

When a couple knows how to properly apply the rules of a method to avoid pregnancy, there are many complex reasons why they disregard the rules (Number 2 above). Often the couple is ambivalent about whether or not to have a baby. They may not have clearly discussed their goals and plans for the future. Couples may "take a chance" with the use of a method or become careless in using the method. Sometimes the subconscious desire for a child is very strong and causes a couple not to follow the method correctly, carefully, and consistently. These examples illustrate some of the variables which contribute to the way a couple uses a method. The motivation of each couple is very unique and different. Pregnancies which occur under these circumstances do not mean that the method is unreliable, but that the couple chose to disregard the rules for pregnancy avoidance — for whatever reason.

Natural family planning is often said to be ineffective based on user-variable effectiveness rates (which are lower than method effectiveness rates). One reason for this is that medical professionals, among others, falsely assume that couples cannot develop the self-mastery necessary to practice continence for the avoidance of pregnancy. Dr. Hanna Klaus, a gynecologist, natural family planning expert, and Medical Missionary Sister, responds in the following way: "To read use effectiveness figures as meaning that clients either cannot learn the method, or will not practice it consistently and therefore have an unplanned pregnancy, is to make condescending assumptions about human intelligence or freedom, and to attempt to reduce complex personal decision making to a demographic figure."[2]

The many couples who successfully use natural family planning methods to avoid or achieve pregnancy are testimony to the capacity of human beings to understand and integrate their fertility into their marriage. Natural family planning means accepting yourself, your spouse, and your joint fertility. It means an openness to living and expressing your relationship over time through children. Natural methods are true and effective family planning.

Notes

1. Nona Aguilar, *No-Pill, No-Risk Birth Control,* pp. 231-232.
2. Hanna Klaus, M.D., *Intercom,* "The Distinction Between Method and User Failure of NFP Methods," March, 1980, p. 12.

For Men Only
by Charles Balsam

I see a direct relationship between my struggle to embrace a natural family planning lifestyle and my desire for a sacramental marriage. Marriage *in Christ* means that our struggle to form a union of two-in-one-flesh must embody Christlike qualities such as unconditional love, sacrifice, and self-control.

I believe the complementary nature of man and woman is realized through the manner in which we strive for union. Through our complementary differences we have had to teach each other to love. Sexually, this has meant that my "feminine" side — my capacity for gentleness, nurturing, compassion, and vulnerability — must be developed. My wife can best encourage and support these capacities through her love for me. It is in our complementarity that we are able to live the natural family planning lifestyle and to have a sacramental marriage.

My experience of marital sexuality has been a mixture of pain and redemption. The pain comes in part from the normal struggle of two lovers to "tune in" to each other's needs and fragility. The pain also comes from my own immaturity and from some unrealistic assumptions and expectations. When these expectations go unspoken and are not dealt with mutually, the struggle seems to be compounded. Love takes time. Love needs bridges, not barriers. Sexually, the only barrier I bring to my marriage is my hesitancy to risk. I believe the form of family planning we have chosen has helped me to accept myself and to seek a deeper union with my wife, and this has been redemptive.

My wife once told me that she might not have married me had I insisted on an artificial form of family planning. That's tough love! She invested three and one-half years in our relationship before we married. Being Catholic may have had something to do with it, but she was most concerned about the integrity of her self and our relationship. She had been charting her natural signs of fertility for over two years, and she knew her "self."

Our decision to use natural family planning has led me to take another look at the Catholic teaching on contraception. In the beginning I assumed it was my wife's problem, and I wondered what gave the Church a right to speak on the topic. It was a painful struggle, for I had to die to the illusion that my own feelings were more "true" than the tradition of my faith. I felt there was no difference between family planning methods. I think I was secretly afraid of continence.

I now see that refraining from intercourse is not the same as contraception because, in refraining, there is no intercourse at all. In fact, refraining from intercourse can be a loving act since we both have to continue to nurture the other areas of need for affection in our relationship. To use contraception would be to act against the good of our love and marriage. With natural family planning, we make use of the naturally infertile phases and do not have to choose against the procreative good or alter the meaning of total self-giving. What has all this meant for me as a typically socialized twentieth-century American male?

The difficulty came in discovering that I had placed more emphasis on genital intimacy than relational intimacy. Along with the gift of transmitting life, relational intimacy is also celebrated through sexual intercourse. Our use of a chemical or mechanical contraceptive would represent another barrier we do not need or want.

Since self-mastery is a quality of a maturing person, continence is healthy. The ability to postpone gratification of any physical urge is one aspect that separates the human person from the rest of the animal world. My appetites can control me. Periodic genital continence means I have to gratify the relational need. It means I have to make a deliberate, conscious, reflective effort to continue to maintain the quality of our relationship. It is a mutual journey. In my struggle, I have had to become more emotionally intimate and more vulnerable — two qualities women want in their husbands but which usually are not part of the social upbringing we receive as males. Thus, I see NFP as an important contributor to my ongoing growth as a male and to marital happiness. It has challenged me to self-mastery so that I can freely give my "self."

I believe men must relate to women as persons equal to men in dignity and relate to them in their *totality*. This includes their fertility, which is unique and different from ours. That, however, is exactly what contraception and abortion do not allow us to do. They do not challenge us to integrate our sexuality, our urges, or our attitudes into a mutually responsible relationship. Natural family planning, in contrast, is not chauvinistic; both the man and the woman have to make it work. Becoming involved in this mutual effort, I believe, helps minimize the possibility of taking sex, or my wife, for granted.

Fertility acceptance, through natural family planning, reminds me of my procreative potential. It is also a constant reminder that genital intimacy is an expression of, not a substitute for, relational intimacy. During each cycle, we experience a "courtship" of sorts. This is extremely important to me, as a male, given my natural tendency to focus only on the quality of the genital relationship or to believe that my wife exists just to please me.

Can I guarantee anything beneficial for you should you choose to use natural family planning? It all depends on your attitudes and the quality of your relationship. NFP calls for self-mastery, self-giving, and self-revelation. Unity is a natural by-product of this. What I am saying is that natural family planning is more than just a birth control method. It is a lifestyle. It is an intimate form of communication, the knowing and sharing of ourselves with each other.

I see how NFP has had a positive effect on me and my marriage in several ways. It has challenged me to question my assumptions about woman as mate and lover. It has also led me to begin appreciating the "feminine" aspects of myself. NFP has taught me about the beauty of the female fertility cycle. I am acutely aware of the difference between cherishing and merely desiring my wife.[1] I have not "arrived" at a perfected or final level of maturity, but I know I am not the same person I was when I married.

Last but not least, NFP has enhanced my appreciation of creation and of God's wisdom in providing us with the potential of transmitting human life while we grow together in unity of body and spirit.

Notes

1. Terrie Guay, *The Personal Fertility Guide,* p. 12.

A Shared Decision, A Shared Responsibility

Christian marriage is an intimate partnership of life and love, a sacrament of mutual and total self-giving. Partnership calls for shared decisions and shared responsibilities. Couples frequently make mutual decisions and share responsibilities about finances, parenting, housing, spousal roles, household chores, family holidays, and the like. Until recently, family planning has been viewed as the sole responsibility of the wife and her doctor. Christian marriage dictates, however, that decisions and responsibilities about fertility and family planning belong to *both* husband and wife.

Natural family planning best exemplifies this description of Christian marriage. Both husband and wife share the responsibility for fertility and decisions about family planning.

Perhaps the following questions will identify some of the values you bring to your relationship:

- To what is God calling us in our marriage?
- How may children do we want to have?
- How can we remain open to these questions throughout our reproductive years?
- How do we value children in relation to material things: money, possessions, social status, etc.?
- How important is the physical, psychological, or spiritual impact of a family planning method on our relationship?
- How generous can we be with life?

As a couple, your decision-making about family planning requires prayer and a reverence for and an openness to God's creative presence in your lives. You must be able to talk honestly and lovingly about the value you place on children and on a Christian family. It is important to remember that conception is a logical and beautiful result of your covenantal love. Children are the living manifestation of your love in-the-flesh.

Fertility is a gift from God, and you are called to be generous with this gift. Family size is not just an issue of economics, but rather a matter of faith.

We urge you to reflect upon and discuss all these issues in a faith context. We are called to be generative and fruitful people. Fertility is the avenue through which we join our will to the creative intentions of God. It is the way we continue to call into being other human persons who become the image and likeness of God in the world. If fertility is an integral part of human dignity, then it follows that every child is a unique, unrepeatable person. Children represent our belief that life is worth living, and that the fullness of the kingdom of God is yet to come.

Page 46 of this booklet contains a worksheet. It is an opportunity for you as a couple to discuss family planning, your relationship as sexual persons, and your expectations within the context of Christian marriage. We hope that this booklet, along with your responses to the worksheet, contributes to an honest, healthy understanding as you make mutual, conscientious decisions about family planning.

Finally, we offer a prayer for Christian parenthood. We urge you to pray it frequently as a couple and reflect on its meaning, most especially when you feel called by God to cooperate with his creative love in bringing new life and new hope into the world.

God our Father, all parenthood comes from you. Allow us to share in that power which is yours alone. Help us to see in the children you send us living signs of your presence in our home. Bless our love and make it fruitful so that new voices may join ours in praise of you, new hearts love you, and new lives bear witness to you. (Author unknown.)

What Does the Catholic Church Teach?

Most people are aware of the fact that the Roman Catholic Church does not endorse all of the family planning methods presented in this booklet. This section is an explanation of the reasoning behind Church teaching.

We urge you to read this section carefully and with an open heart. It is important to realize that the Church's concern for the moral aspects of family planning is not simply a set of rules. Church teaching is ensured by Jesus' promise of the guidance of his Spirit. Even though there is not adequate space here to go into great detail about Church teaching, a few remarks are in order.

In continuity with Church teaching, the Second Vatican Council (1962-1965) asserted that the manner in which human life is transmitted must be determined by objective standards. These standards are "based on the nature of the human person and his acts" in order to "preserve the *full sense* of *mutual self-giving* and *human procreation* in the context of true love."[1] The phrase "full sense" means that conjugal intercourse, the language of marital love, is the symbol and expression of a covenant relationship — an open-ended, vulnerable commitment to an exclusive, life-giving marital union. Thus, we are speaking primarily of the *meanings* of intercourse as well as its potential "effects" — unity and parenthood. Let us briefly focus, then, on these two fundamental aspects of which the Council spoke: the nature of the human person, in light of the call to self-giving that is marriage, and the nature of conjugal intercourse.

The Human Person

Our Christian faith tells us that sexuality, our uniqueness as male or female, is God's gift to us. Pope John Paul II, citing Genesis 2:23-24, says that man and woman are created for unity. They become "one flesh" through a choice, the free gift of themselves. Christian tradition holds that a sacramental marriage begins when two persons express their consent to give and receive the person of the other. This mutual consent, spoken in the vows, is the forming of an "intimate partnership of married life and love . . . structured . . . on the model of His [Christ's] union with the Church."[2] This consent means commitment to the primary and equally important meanings of marriage — the procreation and education of children and the unity of the spouses.

In the light of mutual consent and self-giving, sexuality serves human life and human relationships. The marital relationship is fundamentally a commitment of the whole person — mind and heart, body and spirit. For Pope John Paul, sexuality and the human person are one reality. He speaks of the person as an *"incarnate spirit . . .* a soul which expresses itself in a body. . . . Love includes the human body, and the body is made a sharer in spiritual love."

He adds that " . . . sexuality . . . is by no means something purely biological, but concerns the *innermost being* of the human person . . . .[3] Since human fertility is designed to generate a human person, it surpasses the purely biological level. Human fertility must also be seen as a part of personal identity, relational values, and the gift of the whole person to another in the covenant of marriage.

Conjugal Intercourse

Marital intercourse is a natural sacrament. It is a sign of the wisdom of God's design for human persons. It is a symbol, an expression of two human beings who have vowed to openness, the vulnerability, the *mutual self-giving* of covenant love.

There are two inherent meanings in the marriage act: the procreative and the unitive. The *key* issue is the Church's concern with the morality of deliberately removing or altering the procreative meaning. To intervene, to remove the procreative meaning/potential of intercourse is also to change the *personal and unitive* nature of this loving act.

Is the Church Inconsistent?

According to method effectiveness studies cited earlier in this booklet, it is clear that modern methods of natural family planning are as effective, or more effective, in avoiding pregnancy as artificial methods of birth control. After studying this data, some people assume that natural methods are simply an alternate form of contraception. They further conclude that the Church is inconsistent in promoting only natural methods of fertility acceptance while condemning artificial methods that have the same result.

It is true that in both cases the probable effect — avoiding pregnancy — can be the same. There is a fundamental difference, however, between the two forms of family planning.

It is wrongly supposed that Church teaching opposes contraception because it is used to avoid pregnancy, or because it is most often artificial. Avoiding pregnancy can be good, responsible, or even necessary for married couples. The Church is convinced, however, that certain ways of avoiding pregnancy are morally flawed. These methods compromise the very meaning of marriage and marital intercourse. The use of contraception is an attempt to re-design the nature of marital intercourse by eliminating its procreative meaning and trivializing the promise of total self-giving and mutual acceptance.

Couples who choose artificial methods of birth control are making a statement about the value and the meaning of procreation in relation to their marital love. By their action they imply that conception is merely a biological process and that the birth control method affects only their reproductive capacity. They attempt to separate or exclude the reality of their fertility from their total human personhood. They can lose sight of the fact that as human persons they are a wondrous unity of body and spirit. One author explains this by stating:

"In the marital act, husband and wife are 'speaking' through their body language. . . . They are not simply 'using' their bodies as objects. . . . The truth of the marital act is that it is a reciprocal gift of one's total self. It is a gift which, being total, necessarily includes the procreative potential. Since fertility is an integral element of each spouse, it must be given and received (in so far as it is present) in the marital act. . . .

"To remove the procreation dimension . . . is to introduce the language of rejection and non-acceptance into the act. The marital act is then reduced to an act of manipulation and acceptance-only-with-some-reservations."[4]

By using artificial contraception, couples attempt to eliminate the procreative dimension from their act of intercourse. In other words, they willingly attempt to eliminate God's creative presence from their act of love, from the gift of fertility, and from the goodness of their procreative potential. Their action "is directly aimed against the realization of the procreative good. One is simply not declining to promote that good; one is taking positive steps directly against it."[5]

On the other hand, couples who choose to use natural methods of family planning can be said to both accept and integrate their joint fertility into their covenant love, symbolized by the sex act. They do not reject God's possible creative presence in intercourse.

By avoiding fertile intercourse, "the couple is simply not performing an action whose nature is ordained to elicit God's creative act. God is still present, still respected, but no invitation is sent Him that would invite His presence in the specific form of being a creator of new life."[6]

By contrast, contraception sends the message that God's creative presence is not wanted and that fertility is a biological "problem" rather than a personal gift to be respected as a blessing from God. The Church teaches that couples who practice natural methods can have intercourse during naturally infertile phases and still not be making a conscious choice against the good of procreation. These naturally infertile (non-contraceptive) acts of intercourse still have a procreative *meaning* and value, even though, due to God's design, they do not have a procreative *capacity* or result.

To say it another way, couples who employ fertility acceptance methods (natural family planning) acknowledge God's creative power but choose, by their periodic continence, not to enlist that power. They do not reject God's creative presence in their sexual love, but simply choose not to utilize the procreative potential. Such couples, seeking to avoid pregnancy through selective intercourse, understand that they bring themselves entirely to the sex act. Nothing is done to render sex sterile, make it incomplete, or prevent implantation of a fertilized ovum (a developing human being).

The Church's support for natural methods affirms its teaching that marriage is the mutual giving and receiving of two persons in Christ. This means that the reciprocal giving and receiving is not just spiritual or psychological, but also physical, of which fertility is a part. Natural family planning fosters this integral understanding of Christian marriage. Through a fertility acceptance lifestyle, a married couple using natural family planning affirms the values of personal, bodily and spiritual integrity, and mutual self-giving in union with the Creator and his design.

Therefore, if Pope John Paul's definition of the human person is correct and if covenantal love is the mutual self-giving of two whole persons, it follows that contraception is an objectively contradictory reality. It attempts to eliminate the procreative meaning of marital love from the symbol of self-giving. It trivializes sex and the covenantal promises of marriage, namely the *complete* sharing of one's self and one's life with each other.

This quotation from Pope John Paul summarizes the ideas presented in this section:

" . . . the innate language that expresses the total reciprocal self-giving of husband and wife is overlaid, through contraception, by an objectively contradictory language, namely, that of not giving oneself totally to the other. This leads . . . to a falsification of the inner truth of conjugal love, which is called upon to give itself in personal totality.

"When, instead, by means of recourse to periods of infertility, the couple respect the inseparable connection between the unitive and procreative meanings of human sexuality, they are acting as 'ministers' of God's plan and they 'benefit from' their sexuality according to the original dynamism of 'total' self-giving, without manipulation or alteration.

"In the light of the experience of many couples and of the data provided by the different human sciences, theological reflection is able to perceive and . . . study further the difference . . . between contraception and recourse to the rhythm [here the pope is referring to NFP] *of the cycle:* It is a difference *which is much wider and deeper than is usually thought, one* which involves in the final analysis two irreconcilable concepts of the human person and of human sexuality. *The choice of the natural rhythms* [here the pope is referring to NFP] *involves accepting the cycle of the person, that is, the woman, and thereby accepting* dialogue, reciprocal respect, shared responsibility and self-control. . . . *In this way sexuality is respected and promoted in its truly and fully human dimension and*

is never 'used' as an 'object' that, by breaking the personal unity of soul and body, strikes at God's creation itself at the level of the deepest interaction of nature and person.''[7]

Pope John Paul addresses many deep and complex issues in his writing. It requires much prayer, patience, and reflection to fully grasp the values to which he is pointing.

NFP: A Special Language of Love

After all the positive and negative arguments have been made, there remains one authoritative source: married couples themselves. Research from Shivanandan (1979), Aguilar (1980), the Couple-to-Couple League Study (1985), and others reveals that natural family planning couples are the best witnesses to its positive value and impact on marital intimacy. Many couples will admit that NFP requires growth in self-control, self-sacrifice, dying to self, and other virtues needed by those who wish to follow Christ. Seen in this light, genital abstinence or continence is not merely a strategy or a technique for avoiding conception. It is a necessity for subduing one's tendency toward selfishness and developing the virtue of self-mastery. Far from being anti-sexual, continence enables a couple to embrace intercourse as a special language of total and reciprocal self-giving. Research also shows that couples who abandon contraceptives for fertility acceptance methods are the most adamant about the difference between the two lifestyles. They see their contraceptive-free life as being filled with faith in God the Creator who enables them to love each other and their children more deeply.

This outlook fully supports the prophetic concern of the Church for the integrity of marital intercourse and fertility acceptance. Church teaching has highlighted the values of "dialogue, reciprocal respect, shared responsibility, and self-control." To this should be added the qualities of mutuality, intimacy, and bonding.

These values are involved not only in the effectiveness and acceptance of the natural family planning lifestyle but also in sacramental marriage.

Notes

1. *The Documents Of Vatican II,* "Pastoral Constitution on the Church in the Modern World," #51. America Press, New York, NY, 1966.
2. Ibid., #48.
3. Pope John Paul II, *On the Family (Familiaris Consortio),* Part Two, 11.
4. M. Fightlin, *International Review of Natural Family Planning,* Vol. IX, #2, Summer, 1985, p. 129.
5. Rev. Ronald Lawler, O.F.M. Cap., Joseph Boyle, and William E. May, *Catholic Sexual Ethics.* Our Sunday Visitor, Inc., Huntington, IN, 1985, p. 161.
6. Donald DeMarco, *International Review of Natural Family Planning,* Vol. X, Spring, 1986, p. 67.
7. Pope John Paul II, *On the Family (Familiaris Consortio),* Part Two, 32.

Seeking the Truth and Embracing It

In our secular culture, the birth control issue often is looked upon with a rather pragmatic attitude of "use what is most effective no matter the cost." The prevalence of abortion-on-demand, often as a back-up for contraceptive failure, is a reflection of this attitude. While a Christian attitude includes the need for being responsible, this notion of responsibility does not derive simply from "common sense" or an attitude of "the end justifies the means." The Christian attitude toward contraception and family planning derives from what we are called to do and who we are called to become in Christ. Decisions about family planning must be situated in this faith context.

For the Catholic Christian, conscience is formed by prayerful reflection on the pertinent scriptural passages and Church teachings that serve as the primary indicators of God's will. A well-formed conscience enables us to make responsible decisions by seeking the truth and embracing it. This section assumes that, for those who are seriously probing the Christian meaning of marital sexuality, Church teaching is not merely one option among a variety of value systems. Rather, Church teaching is the fundamental basis of conscience formation.

In the context of marriage, the Church views sexuality as an essential part of the way a human being establishes the most intimate and basic relationships in life: (1) the relationship to one's own body and emotions, (2) to one's spouse, and (3) to the next generation in procreation.

These relationships are revelatory; they reveal something about God. We are God's children, and the relationships within the Trinity — Father, Son, and Spirit — are analogous to a family of love. Therefore, the Church is not concerned just with sex for its own sake; it is concerned with sex as a central dimension in the network of human life, and it views sexual ethics as critical to the living of a Christian life. Sexual ethics is an essential dimension of the ethics of authentic love.

With these points in mind, let us take a brief look at how the Church defines responsible parenthood, one of the important callings of sacramental marriage. We will also touch on conscience formation and moral decision making.

Responsible Parenthood

In the encyclical *Humanae Vitae* (1968), Pope Paul VI identifies four "aspects" of responsible parenthood:

1. The "knowledge and respect of" reproductive processes which are integral parts of the human person;
2. The integration of the "tendencies of instinct or passion" with our reason and free will;
3. Consideration of the "physical, economic, psychological and social conditions" in relation to which couples generously decide to have several children or, for serious reasons, to limit their family size;
4. A "profound relationship" with the moral order established by God, through the formation of a "right conscience."[1]

Responsible parenthood implies that couples take into account many different factors when having a family, including the ongoing fruitfulness involved in educating and raising children. In the transmission of life, Catholics are not free to disregard the creative intentions of God. The complementary nature of man and woman, the sex drive and the reproductive faculty, the desire for love and unity — all are mysteries to be lived. These are connected "perspectives" of human relationships, and the transmission of life is an important component. This is why the Church teaches that married couples are to respect this gift and the meaning it has in their overall relationship.

How many children should you responsibly seek to parent? The bishops of the Second Vatican Council address this challenging question. In the *Pastoral Constitution on the Church in the Modern World* they remind married couples that family planning decisions cannot be made arbitrarily or simply on the basis of convenience. Family planning requires decisions of conscience that must respect the law of God and the teaching authority of the Church which authentically interprets divine law. When Christian couples, in a spirit of sacrifice and with trust in divine providence, carry out their duties of procreation with generous, human, and Christian responsibility, they glorify the Creator and find fulfillment in Christ.[2]

In forming your conscience, you need to reflect carefully upon the teaching of the Church as normative for the Catholic Christian.

Conscience Formation

The tradition of the Church emphasizes two key aspects of conscience: "(1) as absolutely fundamental in understanding the dignity of the human person in his or her relationship with God, and (2) as a practical moral guide in making judgments and decisions in daily life."[3] We are called as individuals and as couples to image God's love by the free, mutual and responsible giving of ourselves to each other. For "God does not force the human person to live responsibly and lovingly, but he does invite and call in the depths of each person's heart. Here, 'in the depths of the heart,' is where conscience exists. . . . The dignity of the human person is this: that he or she can intelligently and *freely* choose God's will and God's law."[4]

The American Catholic bishops are aware of the complex nature of the family planning issue and the many reasons people reject Church teaching on the subject. This is why, in 1976, the American bishops issued a statement of concern, which said in part:

" . . . we ask our people not to lose heart or turn away from the community of faith when they find themselves caught in these conflicts. We urge them to seek appropriate and understanding pastoral counsel, to make use of God's help in constant prayer and recourse to the sacraments, and to investigate honestly such legitimate methods of birth limitation as natural family planning."[5]

The above quotation is out of context here, and is neither a substitute nor a basis for conscience formation. It has been quoted to show that the pastoral leaders of the Church are aware of the difficulty in living up to the call. Conscience formation is a lifelong process, of which moral decision making is a major part. In fact, good moral decision making is the goal, the end result, of a well-formed conscience. When it comes to marriage and family life, there are many moral decisions involved in the way you as husband and wife love each other, relate with your children, handle your finances, and so on.

Conscience development is important in order that moral decision making occurs in a correct, reasonable manner. Your conscience is to be formed throughout your life. Time, prayer, consultation, humility, and honesty are required so that you are always seeking the truth of what is best — what is God's will for human life in a given situation.

Conscience can be defined as "one's best judgment as to what, in the circumstances, is the morally right thing to do. . . . it cannot merely be a feeling or a personal decision to act or live in a certain way. . . . Concern for the truth is essential. . . . But conscience does more than reveal the gap between what we are and what we ought to become. It is also a summons to realize our full humanity.

"For one who has Catholic faith, who has acquired a happy, personal certainty that the Lord teaches and guides us in the teaching of the Church, the insistent message of the Catholic faith is not something alien to conscience. . . . Church teaching is there from the beginning in the formation of conscience."[6]

Below is a brief presentation on the steps involved in moral decision making, which is the result of a well-formed conscience.

Steps in Moral Decision Making

1. Define the problem and the effects it is having on persons or situations in your life.
2. Prayerfully study, respect, and heed the guidance of the Church in the matter.
3. Examine the alternatives.
4. Take counsel with several people of various stages and experience in life — people you trust, people who will be truthful and objective with you, perhaps even confrontive.
5. Pray for guidance, humility, wisdom, and mercy.
6. Judge which alternative is morally right. Then choose to do it.
7. Resolve to continue praying about the decision. As a result of your decision, do you have a sense of peace of mind and heart?

It is important to realize that moral decision making is not an overnight process; forming your conscience takes time and must become a pattern in your life. Conscience formation and moral decision making should open you up to yourself. There is a difference between looking for an answer and looking for a justification for what you "feel" is right or have already decided to do. The ongoing formation of your conscience means that you are sincerely open to continuing the inquiry.

Notes

1. Pope Paul VI, *On the Regulation of Birth* (the encyclical *Humanae Vitae*, on marriage and responsible parenthood), 1968, #10.
2. *The Documents of Vatican II,* "Pastoral Constitution on the Church in the Modern World," #50.
3. Daniel L. Lowery, C.SS.R., *Following Christ: A Handbook of Catholic Moral Teaching,* Liguori Publications, 1982, p. 39.
4. Ibid., pp. 39-40.
5. National Conference of Catholic Bishops, *To Live in Christ Jesus: A Pastoral Reflection on the Moral Life,* 1976, II.
6. Lawler, Boyle, and May, *Catholic Sexual Ethics,* pp. 100, 112.

Worksheet

Directions: Make two copies of this worksheet — one for each partner. Take ten to fifteen minutes *apart* from each other. Reflect on the questions and jot down your honest response to each question. Then take time together to review and discuss your answers. (Write your answers on a separate sheet of paper or on a xerox copy of this page.)

1. I would like us to have _____ number of children because . . .

2. How would I like us to achieve our family size?

3. How will I/we know when we are ready to have children/start a family?

4. Who is responsible for our avoiding or achieving pregnancy in our marriage? Woman? Man? Doctor?

5. If, in spite of our best efforts to avoid conception, we became pregnant, I would (think, feel, do, etc.) . . .

6. If I found out we were unable to conceive and bear children, I would . . .

7. What is the relationship between our family planning decision and our Christian faith?

8. Do I feel we both have a good grasp of all forms of family planning? Do I feel at peace about our family planning decisions? Explain.

Other Resources and Suggested Reading

Gary M. Atkinson, M.D., and Albert S. Moraczewski, O.P., *A Moral Evaluation of Contraception and Sterilization: A Dialogical Study.* Pope John XXIII Center, Braintree, MA, 1979.

Clayton Barbeau, *Delivering the Male: Out of the Tough-Guy Trap into a Better Marriage.* Winston Press, Minneapolis, MN, 1982.

Pope John Paul II, *On the Original Unity of Man and Woman: Catechesis on the Book of Genesis.* Daughters of St. Paul, Boston, MA, 1981.

John F. Kippley and Sheila F. Kippley, *The Art of Natural Family Planning.* The Couple to Couple League International, Inc., Cincinnati, OH, Third Edition, 1984.

Hanna Klaus, M.D., *Natural Family Planning: A Review,* Natural Family Planning Center, 8514 Bradmoor Drive, Bethesda, Maryland 20817.

David Knight, *The Good News About Sex.* St. Anthony Messenger Press, Cincinnati, OH, 1979.

John A. Sanford, *The Invisible Partners.* Paulist Press, Ramsey, NJ, 1980.

U.S. Catholic Conference, *Education in Human Sexuality for Christians: Guidelines for Discussion and Planning.* Washington, DC, 1981.

Vatican Congregation for Catholic Education. "Education and Guidance In Human Love." *ORIGINS* December 15, 1983, 13:27, pp. 449-461.

Mercedes Arzu Wilson, *The Ovulation Method of Birth Regulation: The Latest Advances for Achieving or Postponing Pregnancy — Naturally.* Von Nostrand Reinhold Company, New York, NY, 1980.

Resource Centers for Further Information

For additional information on natural family planning, contact any of the following resource centers:

In the United States:

The Couple to Couple League
3621 Glenmore Avenue
P.O. Box 11084
Cincinnati, Ohio 45211
Phone: 513/661-7612

Family of the Americas Foundation, Inc.
(Formerly: WOOMB-USA)
1150 Lovers Lane
P.O. Box 219
Mandeville, Louisiana 70448
Phone: 504/626-7724

Pope Paul VI Institute for the
   Study of Human Reproduction
6901 Mercy Road
Omaha, Nebraska 68106
Phone: 402/390-6600

WOOMB International
Secretariat
8514 Bradmoor Drive
Bethesda, Maryland 20817
Phone: 301/897-9323

In Canada:

SERENA Canada
151 Holland Avenue
Ottawa, Ontario K1Y 0Y2
Canada
Phone: 613/728-6536

Local/Diocesan NFP Information